THE EEL &
THE BLOWFISH

A Graphic Novel of
Dreams, Trauma & Healing

Leanne Domash, PhD & Terry Marks-Tarlow, PhD

The Eel & the Blowfish

Published by IPBooks (International Psychoanalytic Books)
Queens, NY
Online at www.IPBooks.net

For speaking engagements and workshops on topics related to the graphic novel, please contact Leanne Domash at leanne.domash@gmail.com and Terry Marks-Tarlow at markstarlow@hotmail.

Illustrated by Terry Marks-Tarlow (with Leanne Domash)
Cover design by Darby Tarlow
Layout by David Ilan

ISBN: 978-1-956864-12-0

Dear Reader,

We authors/illustrators have been psychotherapists for decades. Day in and day out, we sit with the unspeakable. We feel the shame that trauma survivors and their perpetrators grapple with, especially if their truths remain hidden. This mythic tale is designed to lessen the terror and anxiety of trauma. While our novel is meant to be inspirational and help to resolve suffering, it is important to understand it is not intended to be a substitute for seeking professional psychological or medical guidance.

Along with those of you who have experienced and survived trauma, we also invite your family, friends, and therapists to read these pages to understand your experience and encourage you to find your voice. In fact, all readers interested in trauma will come away with greater awareness, deepened empathy, and heartfelt compassion. As you read the pages ahead, you may find some of the content disturbing. Please notice what happens in your body. If you get triggered or unduly distressed, take a moment to calm yourself before returning to our story.

May this novel gift you the courage to speak. May you laugh and cry with us as your shame dissolves. May these characters open your heart and expand your sense of the possible. May you explore the dark and light corners of your unconscious mind.

With love,
Leanne and Terry

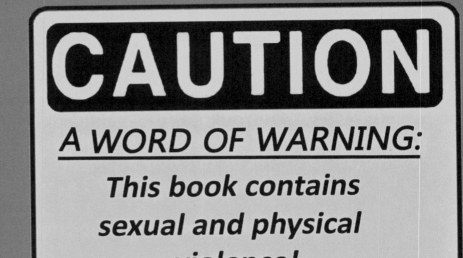

IV

Legend

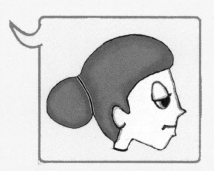

Toni's Mother

Toni, *Our Heroine*

Charlie, *Toni's Brother*

Lulu, *Toni's Friend*

Dr. Young, *Toni's Therapist*

Memory = cloud border

Fantasy = fire border

v

UNDERWATER HELL

Chapter One

12

14

TONI CRACKS OPEN

Chapter Two

17

19

Charlie and I were underwater, drowning. Then I turned into a powerful blowfish. I changed Charlie into an eel, shot my toxins, and blew him to bits.

22

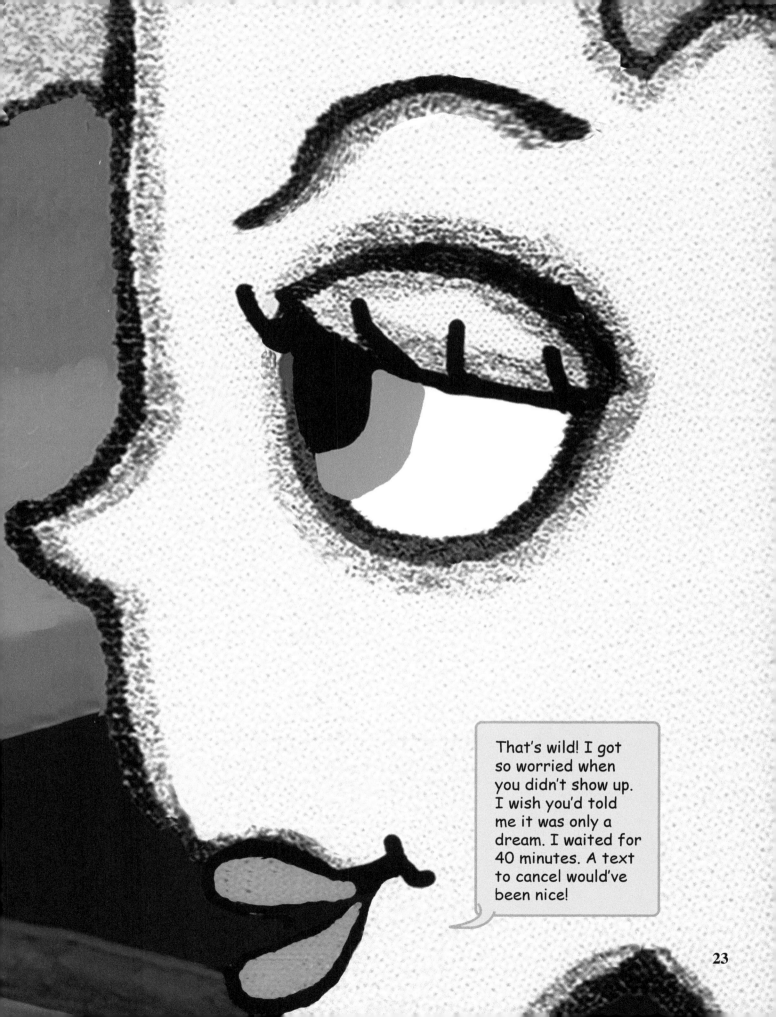

23

 Our connection can bring you into the comfort zone of the "Window of Tolerance." As I just explained to my psychology students, it's the space between being so agitated that you're anxious and so withdrawn that you're depressed.

Hyperarousal Zone

Hypervigilance   Fight   Flight

Comfort Zone

Calm   Connected   Joyful

Hypoarousal Zone

Freeze   Feigned Death   Collapse

Window of Affect Tolerance

31

33

Okay, let's figure out what we can do for you right now.

How about we do a yoga flow together, like child's pose to calm down or a backbend to open our hearts? Want to listen to a Chopin nocturne to reflect or blast Guns & Roses to wake up? Go for a walk to the park to get grounded? Draw our dreams to get into creative flow?

42

43

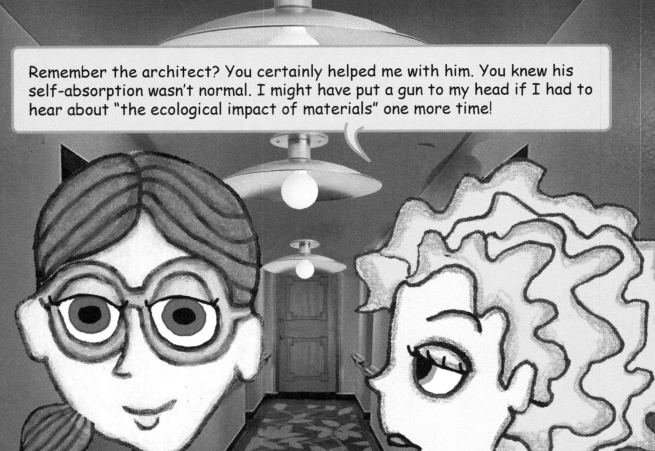

Usually I'm rational, but he agitated me so much that I couldn't think straight. You helped me calm down and break away.

Hyperarousal Zone

Comfort Zone

Hypoarousal Zone

A R O U S A L

Window of Affect Tolerance

48

Between the two of us, we bridge the emotional and analytic. Everyone learns best when they integrate feelings and intuition with logic and reason.

49

50

A cool thing about myths is how they bridge the left and right brain. I'm teaching a course about this right now. Everybody's story reads like a myth. We all share the same set of *archetypes*, those patterns found in every culture.

51

I know you're an academic, but let's get real here. Myths are powerful because we recognize ourselves in them. They help us feel less alone with pain and struggle.

I think that's why my mother loved them so much. Listening to myths inspired me to become a writer—that and the journal I was always scribbling in.

54

55

56

57

IN THERAPY
Chapter Three

59

Maybe together we can lessen your fear.

You're so controlling. I'm really upset!

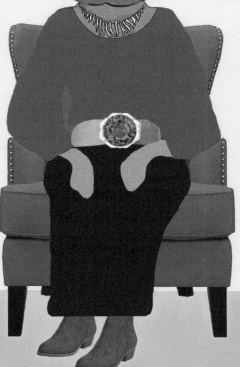

63

NEXT SESSION

66

68

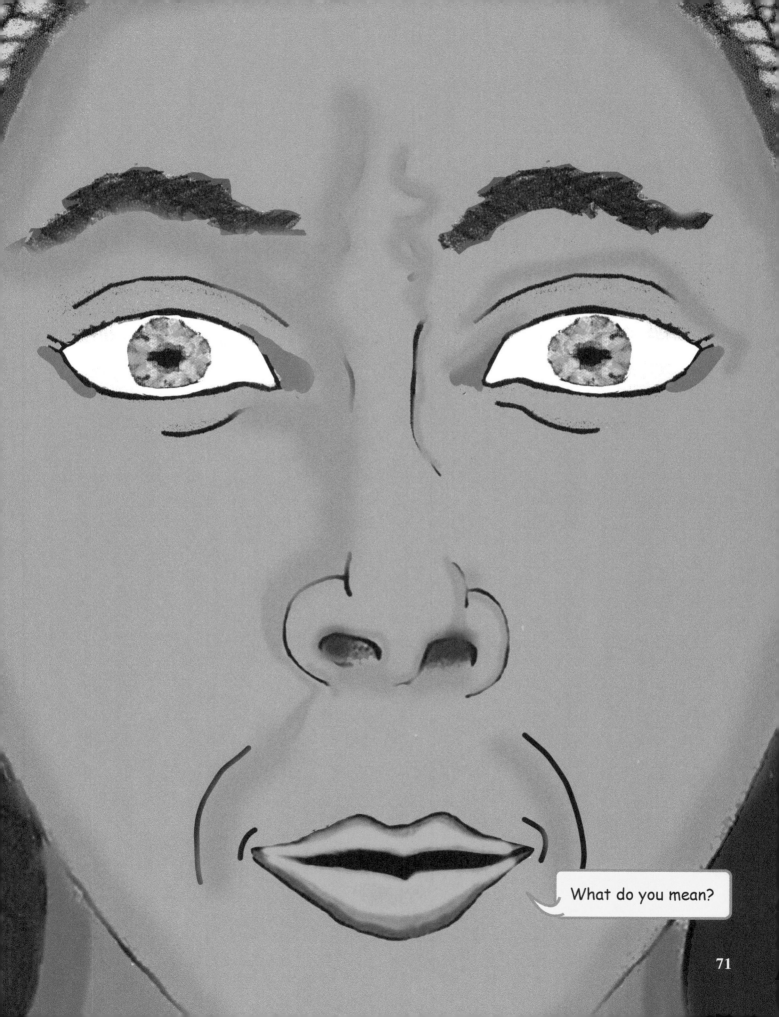

72

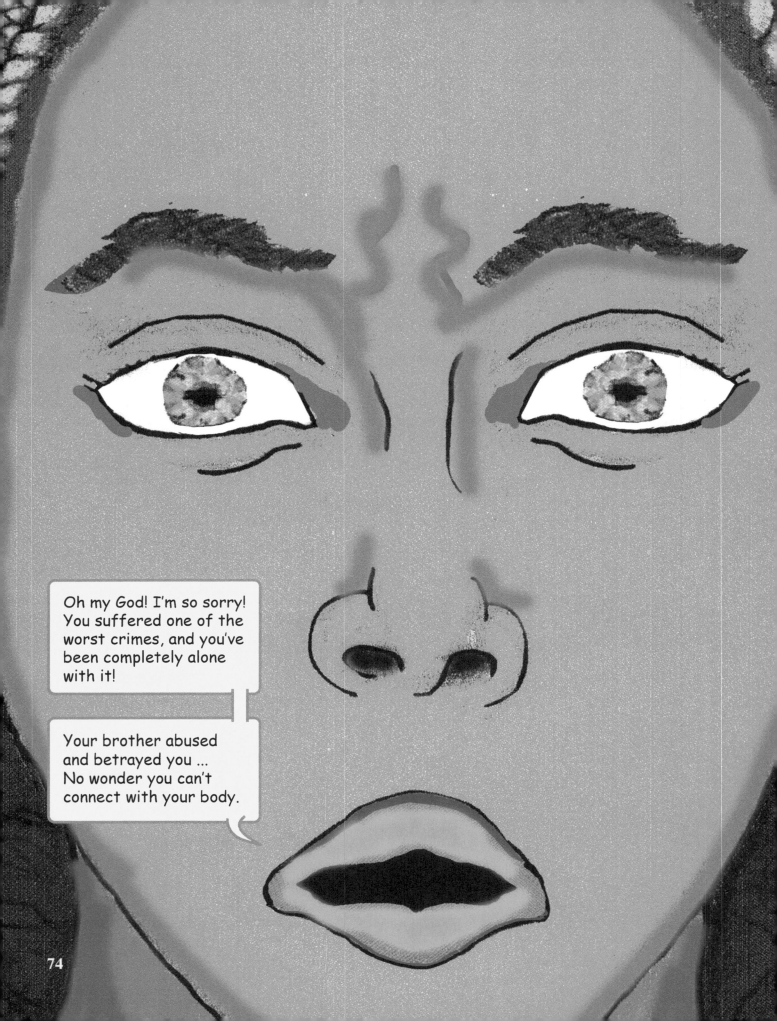

74

75

77

78

81

DREAMWORK

Chapter Four

85

87

88

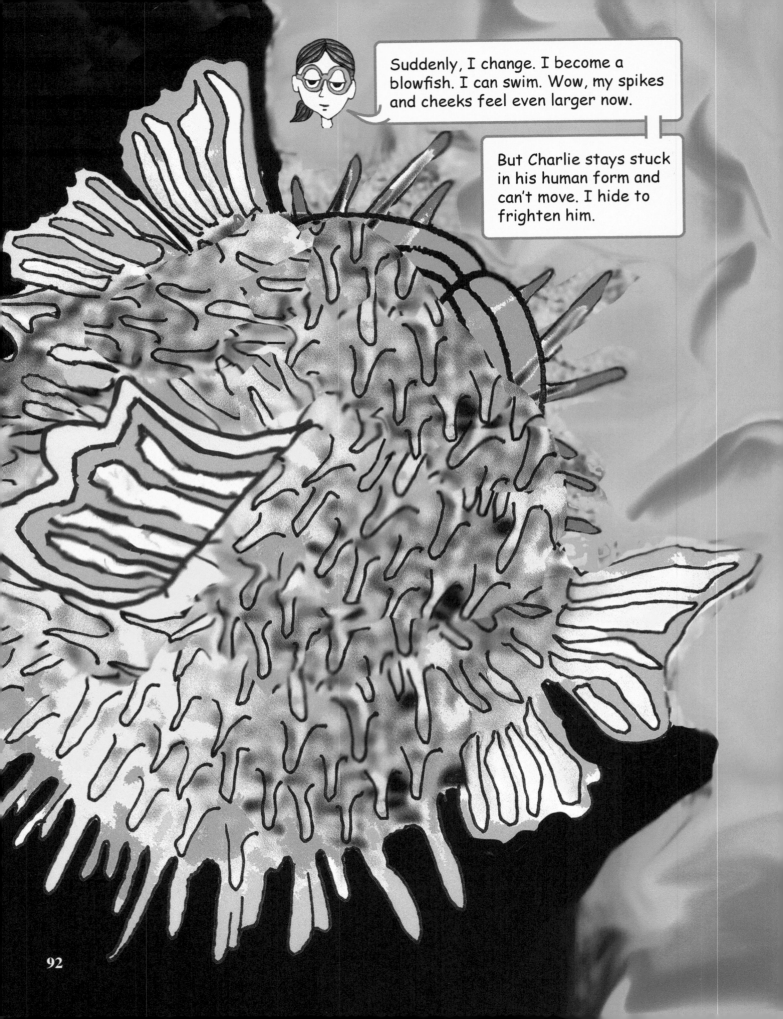

92

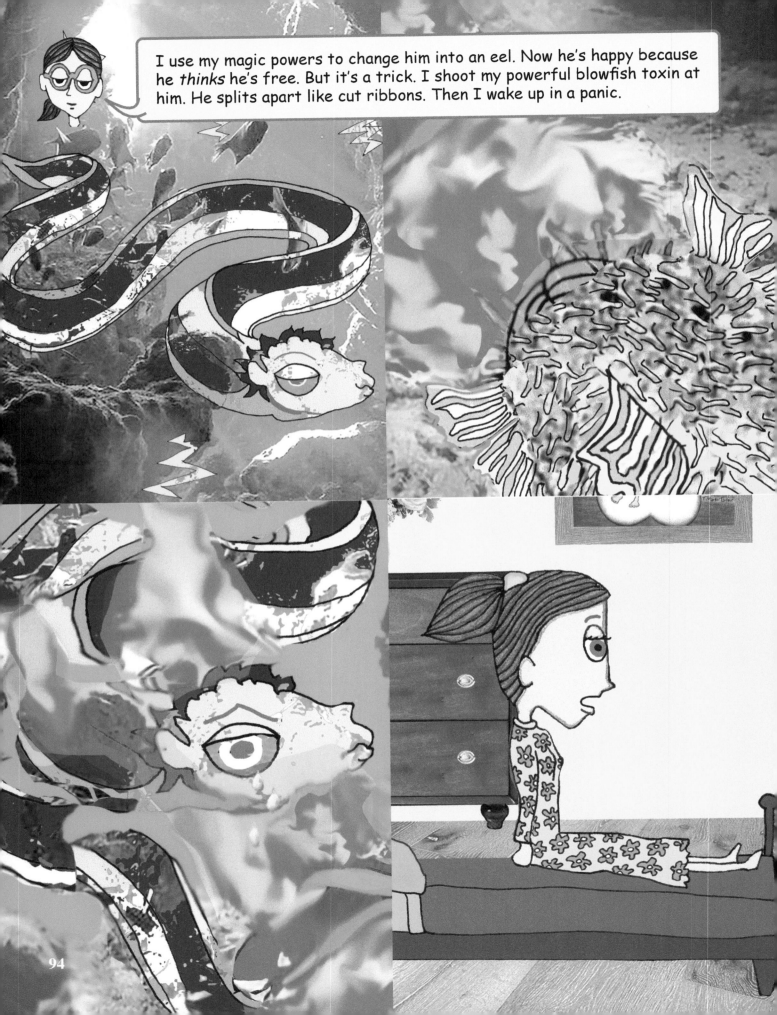

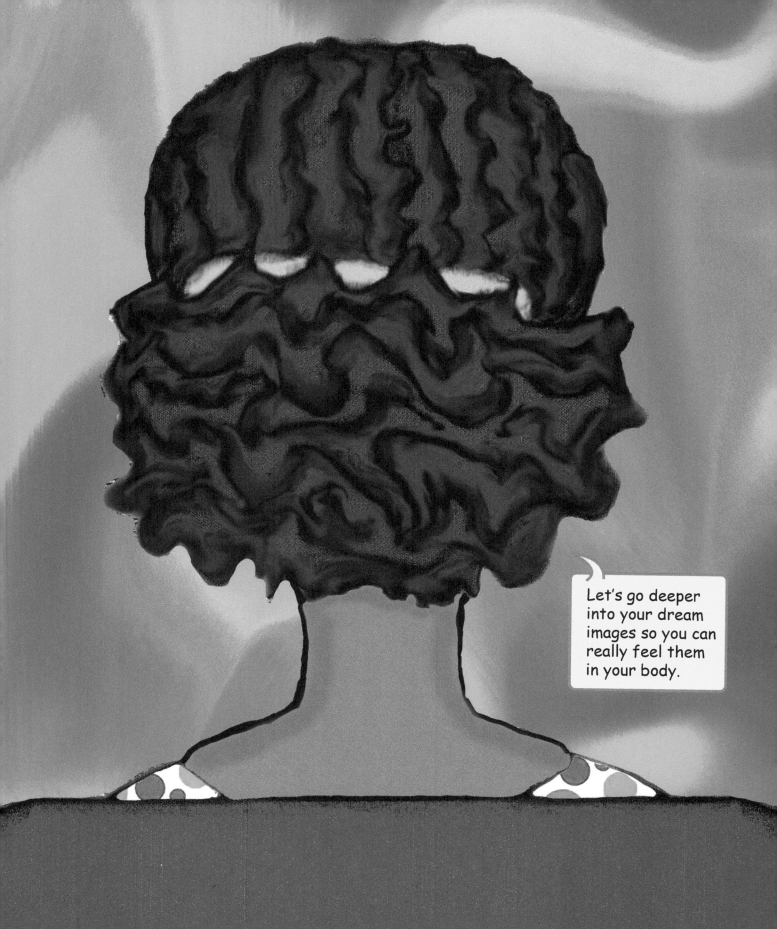

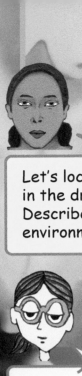

Let's locate you in the dream. Describe the environment.

Very clear blue sea. There are rocks and fish swimming. The water is cold.

How do you feel next to Charlie?

Scared. Where are we? Soon we might not be able to breathe! I know Charlie's beside me, but I can't turn to see him.

100

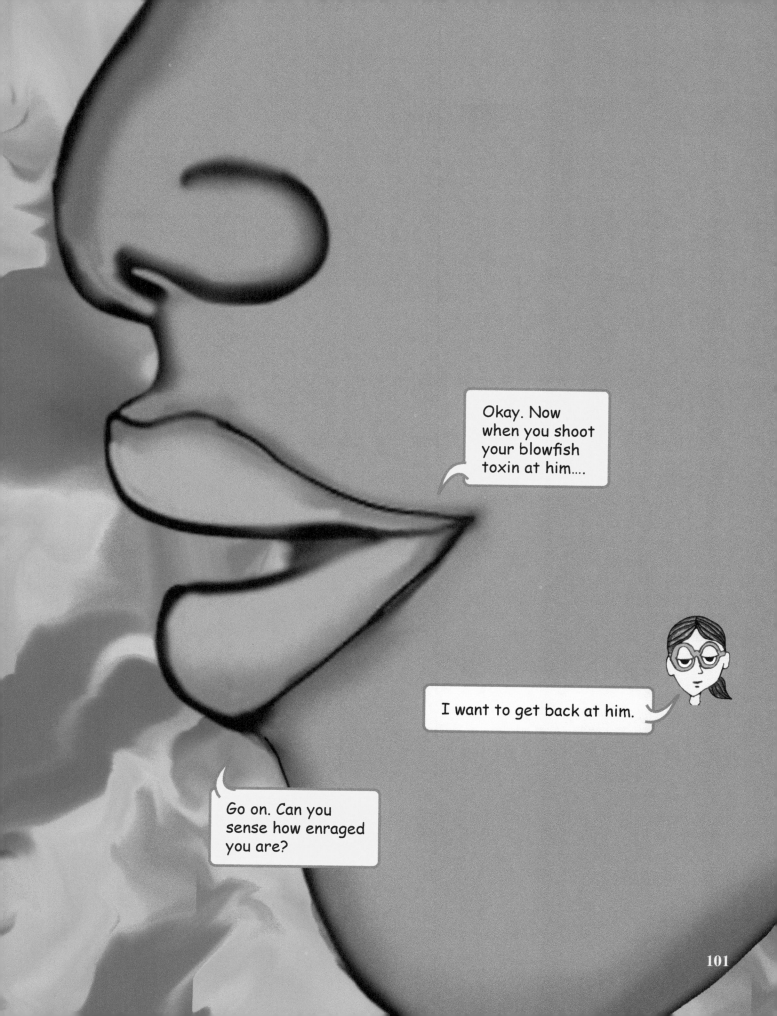

103

106

109

Repeat these images forward and backward in your mind.

Sit with this for a while. Practice the repetition for 10, even 20 minutes scattered throughout the day.

Power

Panic

Fear

Anger

115

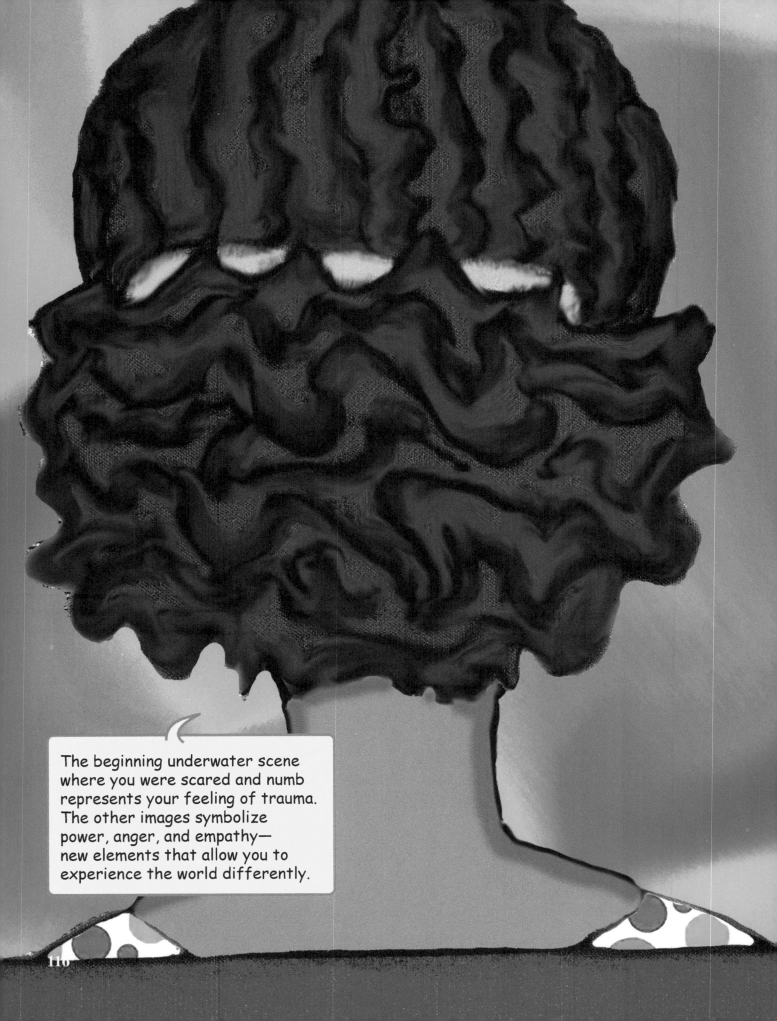

The beginning underwater scene where you were scared and numb represents your feeling of trauma. The other images symbolize power, anger, and empathy— new elements that allow you to experience the world differently.

117

But *your* dream changes the narrative. The combination of old and new, side-by-side helps create new patterns. Finally, we formed a composite of the images.

118

119

NEXT SESSION

121

Do you know about the Chinese dragon? It lives in the clouds and makes rain and stormy weather. Storms represent worldly chaos, but this Trickster also guards otherworldly pearls of enlightenment.

In Chinese culture, chaos is necessary for order and even wisdom to emerge. In your dream, when you shot a toxic cloud at Charlie, you created chaos. You shook things up!

ICE STATUES

Chapter Five

129

133

A songbird flies through the window and circles back and forth between us. The bird's music warms my heart and melts my ice. But Charlie's heart is too hardened. He's frozen solid.

Could Charlie be dead?

135

139

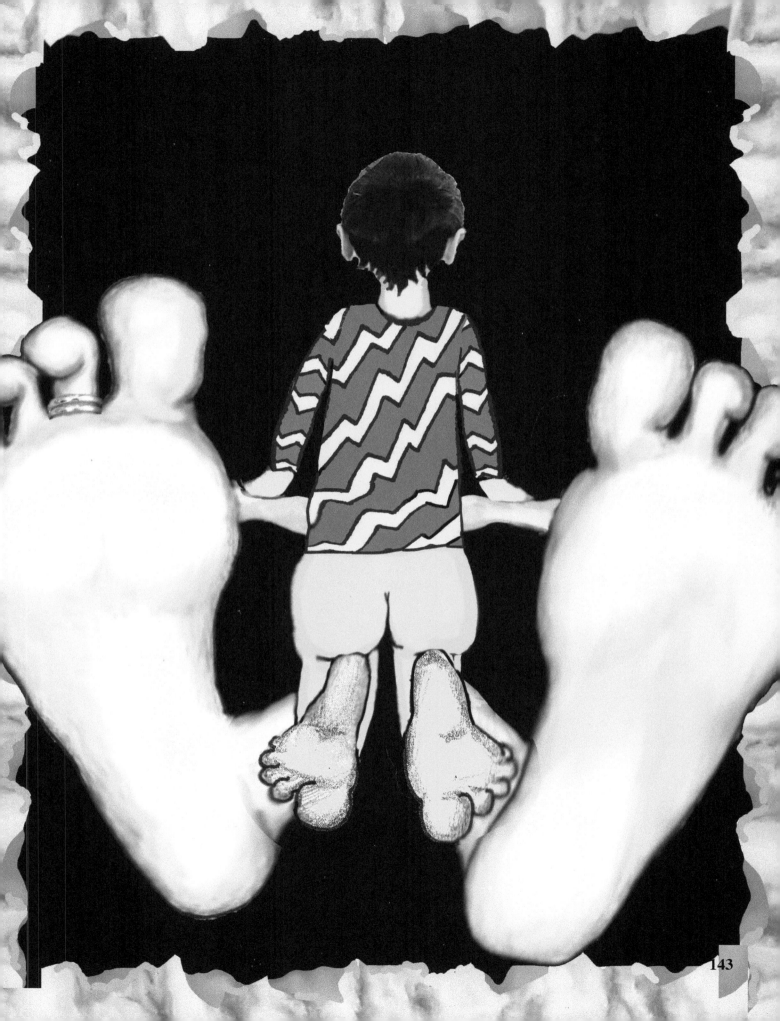

144

Charlie hardly ever looked at me after that. I was only 11 and he 13. That's when he began using drugs and partying. Underneath, *now* I know he was frozen too.

Hyperarousal Zone

Hypoarousal Zone

AROUSAL

Window of Affect Tolerance

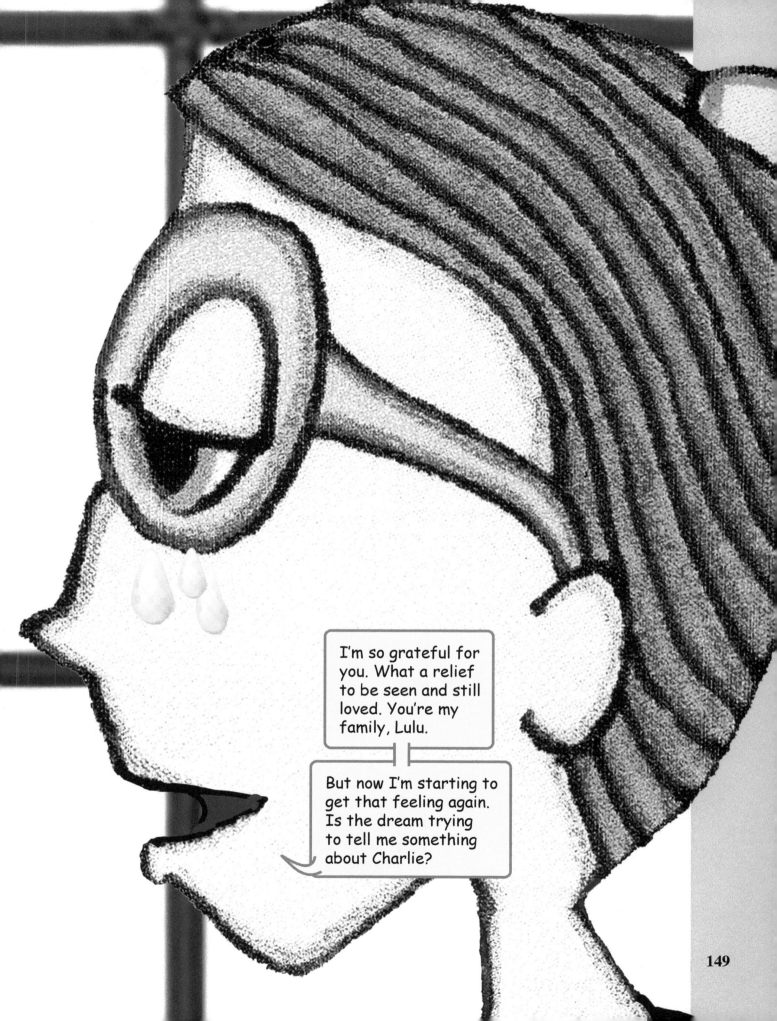

149

151

If Charlie doesn't answer, I think we *have to* find him... Would you come with me?

152

THREE
VARIATIONS
ON A THEME

Chapter Six

155

I see it that way. Three is the archetypal number for *change*. In Snow White, three drops of blood fall on the snow, three birds visit her coffin.

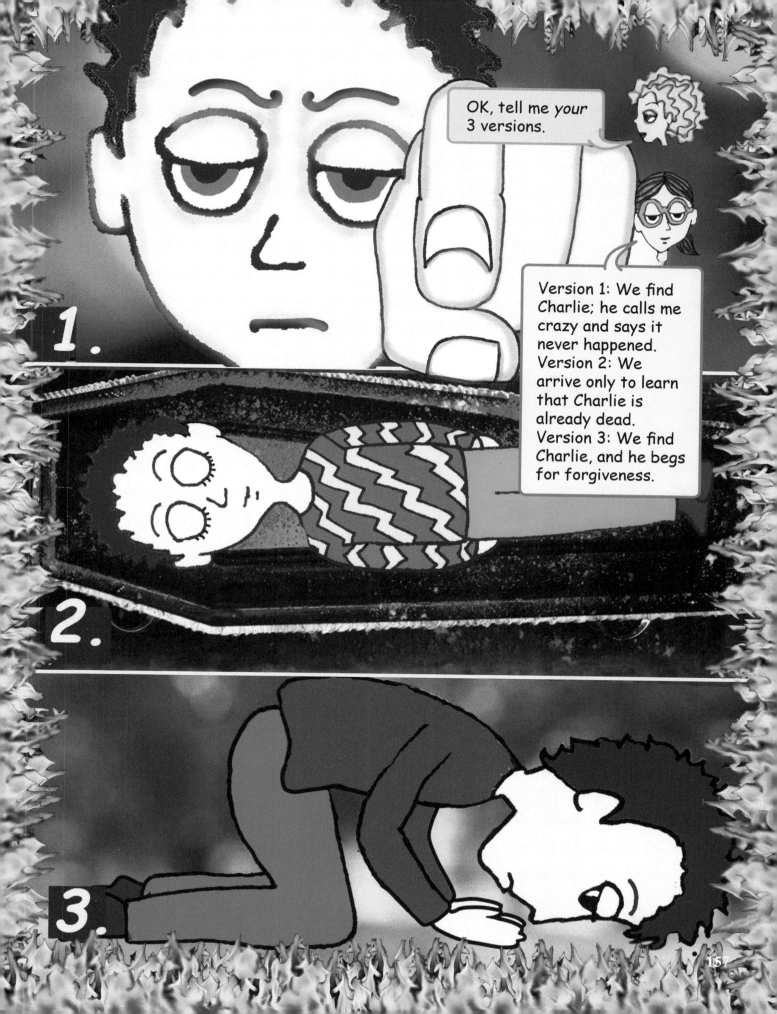

162

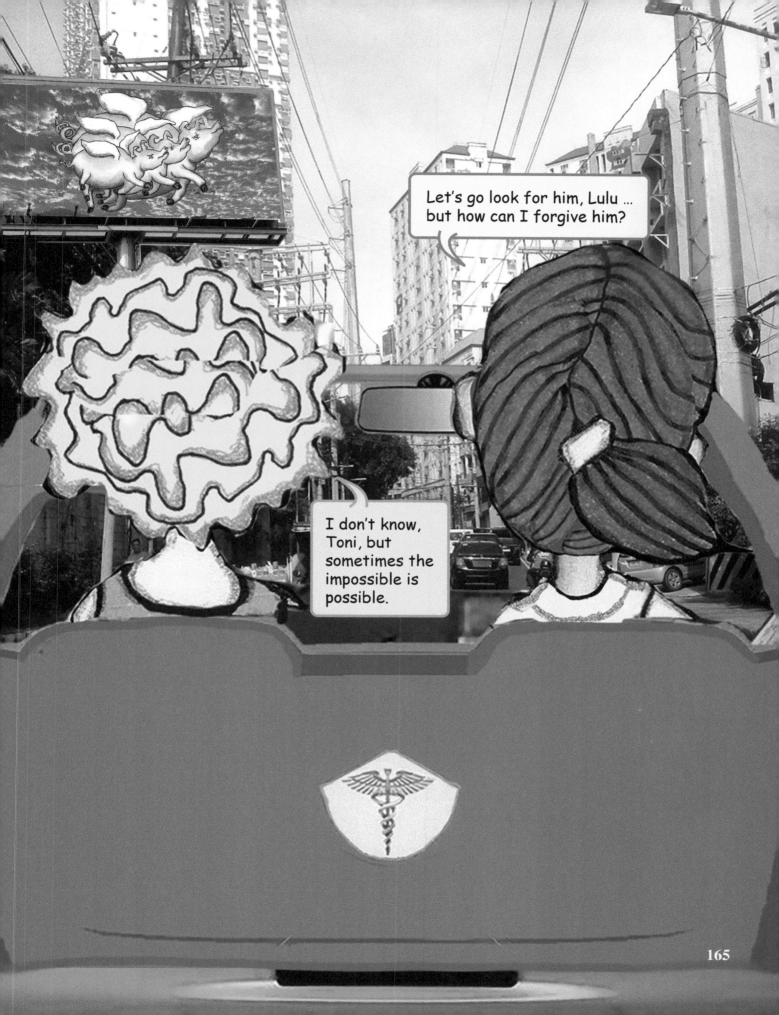

165

173

175

Close your eyes, Charlie. Feel the thread of our connection.

But *how* do I feel it?

Remember how close we were before all that happened.

183

UNDERWATER HEAVEN
Chapter Seven

194

195

But you kept walking and seeking, Charlie. That shows you want to live.

201

THERAPY SESSION

207

209

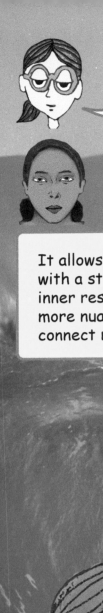

210

Another part of the dream is coming to me. Charlie and I are in the water. He's depressed and I try to cheer him up. I tell him—and I can't believe I said this—that when our time has come and we both line up at the gates of Underwater Heaven, he'll go in ahead of me.

Somewhere I read the mystics say a sinner who repents is holier than one who has never sinned. Can you imagine, after what he did, he gets to go to Heaven first!!

211

It was so weird. We found him on the Golden Gate Bridge, poised to jump. We frantically waved until we caught his attention and I talked him down from the edge.

But even with all your mixed feelings, you saved someone's life. I admire that.

You started today's session with your own dream rather than Charlie's crisis. What a contrast from being so disconnected from yourself just a few weeks ago.

217

When you left, you set a new boundary. You broke the intergenerational pattern of being trapped in abusive relationships. Your mother never broke free from having to placate and take care of your father.

But what's next?

Ending this pattern creates possibilities for a new beginning, including what happens next with Charlie, if anything.

I'm reminded of the ultimate snake image, the Uroborus, the serpent that swallows its own tail. The Uroboros represents self-creation. We all evolve by continually reframing past experiences in light of new ones.

223

AFTERWORD

Toni continues to work through her early trauma in psychotherapy. She stays in sporadic contact with Charlie, and they occasionally get together. Meanwhile, Toni struggles to develop her writing. She is about to have her first short story published.

Lulu continues as a psychology professor but works on becoming less pedantic. She enters a messy relationship that does not end well and keeps trying to unpack what went wrong. She hopes to find a new partner soon.

Charlie struggles to reconnect with the world and find meaning in his day to day. He returns to college and wants eventually to work with victims and perpetrators of sex crimes.

Acknowledgements

Special thanks to Darby Tarlow for her careful, gendered critique of multiple drafts of the manuscript. We are extremely grateful to David Ilan for his artistic eye in formatting this book. Thanks to Sandy Brown for keeping the psychotherapy process authentic, to Pelle Nordin for valuable help with character development, and to Katthe Wolf for her deep understanding, expansive mindset, insightful observations, and wise suggestions. We also want to acknowledge the following readers for their careful attention to drafts: Kristina Cordero, Georgianne Cowan, Tom Goren, Robert Grossmark, Karin Hart, Alan Kintzer, Wayne Lehrer, Pamela McCrory, Louise Rosager, Peter Rysavy, Rachel Paula Shapiro, Jarred Sharar, Alok Srivastava, Barbara Suter, Buz Tarlow, Ken Theil, and Susan Warshow.

We could not have spent years toiling over the details without the kind and loving support of our families and close friends.

Leanne and Terry also thank the songbird for bringing pearls of wisdom and thank Toni for demonstrating how symbols evolve.

Resources

For more information and resources, visit https://www.eelandblowfish.com/

BOOKS

Bosnak, R. (1998). *A Little Course in Dreams*. Boston, MA: Shambhala.

Bosnak, R. (2008). *Embodiment: Creative Imagination in Medicine, Art and Travel*. New York, NY: Routledge.

Ogden, P., Minton, K., & Pain, C. (2006). *Trauma and the Body: A Sensorimotor Approach to Psychotherapy.* New York, NY: Norton.

Scaer, R. (2014). *The Body Bears the Burden: Trauma, Dissociation and Disease.* New York, NY: Routledge.

Schore, A. (2019). *Right-Brain Psychotherapy.* New York, NY: Norton.

van der Kolk, B. (2014).*The Body Keeps the Score: Brain, Mind, and Body in the Healing of Trauma.* New York, NY: Penguin.

ORGANIZATIONS

Be Strong Families

National Alliance for Mental Illness (NAMI)

National Center for PTSD

Survivors of Incest Anonymous: A 12-Step Program

CPSIA information can be obtained
at www.ICGtesting.com
Printed in the USA
BVHW021449311022
650754BV00006B/45